MW01595110

GET UP AND GET DRESSED

*A WOMAN'S GUIDE TO LOOKING AND FEELING
POWERFUL ACCORDING TO GOD'S IMAGE*

Shaquanna Chappelle

Copyright © 2020 Shaquanna Chappelle Enterprises, LLC.

All rights reserved. No part of this publication may be reproduced, distributed, or transmitted in any form or by any means, including photocopying, recording, or other electronic or mechanical methods, without the prior written permission of the publisher, except in the case of brief quotations embodied in critical reviews and certain other noncommercial uses permitted by copyright law. For permission requests, please email me@shaquannachappelle.com.

ISBN: 978-0-578-72011-1

Front cover image by Howell Design Studios

Book design by Seriously Creative Designs

Edited by Speak Write Play, LLC

Printed by BookLogix

Printed in the United States of America

www.shaquannachappelle.com

Although this publication is designed to provide accurate information in regard to the subject matter covered, the publisher and the author assume no responsibility for errors, inaccuracies, omissions, or any other inconsistencies herein. This publication is meant as a source of valuable information for the reader; however, it is not meant as a replacement for direct expert assistance. If such level of assistance is required, the services of a competent professional should be sought.

For my angel, Wanda E. Starks.
My first example of grace, confidence, and faith that will
live within me forever.

Acknowledgements

Get Up and Get Dressed is a product of my obedience to and faith in God. From the day He placed it on my heart to produce this book, God has held my hand the entire time. I give God all of the glory for providing the vision, ideas, words, wisdom, and resources. Thank you God, for being the source of my strength and provider of my peace as I completed this assignment.

To my angel in heaven, my Queen. You are the woman I envision standing beside God cheering me on as He guides my every step. Mommy, thank you for teaching me the power of a well-dressed woman who walks, talks, and loves like Jesus Christ. You've made this possible, and I will continue to make you proud.

Bryan, there aren't enough words to describe how much you've played an integral part in the production of yet another project of mine. Thank you for granting me the space to write freely, while always giving me the encouraging push to stay committed and finish strong. You know how much this book means to me. I love you and appreciate the man you are in my life.

Thank you Daddy and Margie for your unwavering support. You continue to stand in my corner with every journey set before me. I'm grateful for your advice and guidance that have been penned in the pages of my book. I know this will make you proud of the woman you raised.

Krystina, Morgan, and Lea, my life is incomplete without having my sisters behind me every step of the way. Thank you for cheering me on and holding me accountable throughout this entire process.

To The Sequel, our love and sisterhood is immeasurable. Thank you for always having my back, showing up, and being only a call, text, or group chat away. I love you all deeply. (And thanks LaToya C. for contributing your expertise!)

Special thanks to Dr. Ward-Porter for creating a safe space for me to heal, process, grieve, and just be me. I credit you for the growth and maturity shown in this book.

Thank you Angela, Latoya M., and Lauryn for being the best prayer and accountability partners. I appreciate you for being my sounding boards and speaking honestly on this path to purpose.

To my editor Ethleen of Speak Write Play, LLC, thank you for helping me articulate the exact message that will greatly impact women.

Lakia "LB" Brandenburg, you've been my inspiration from the start. I appreciate being connected to you. Thank you for everything!

To all my past and current clients, you inspire me more than you know. You all are beautiful, powerful, and stylish women who continue to walk boldly in your purpose. I love you all!

And finally, to every supporter, thank you for seeing me. Thank you for believing in me. I continue to pray for every woman connected to me. I don't take your support lightly.

Table of Contents

Introduction

"I'm uncomfortable with my body and don't feel confident in my appearance, so I always dress to hide myself," the woman in my group said.

My heart immediately dropped. We were sitting in an auditorium at a women's conference having a general conversation about our passions. After explaining to this complete stranger what I specialized in, she shared how, throughout her life, she was always insecure about the way she looked. She felt like she wasn't good enough to stand out, so she always settled for clothing that made her blend in with the crowd.

"How long have you been feeling like this?" I asked.

"All of my life."

During my drive home, I couldn't let this woman's words go. I knew how the way I dressed powerfully fueled me with the confidence to break through any feelings of self-doubt or insecurities. I understood firsthand how it felt to not think you're good enough to stand out and be noticed. My passion for helping women overcome their struggles with their confidence was ignited even greater than before.

I often come across women who want to dress better or switch up their style so they can feel better about their appearance. However, there's one thing that tends to be ignored and missed: the underlying confidence that shapes the woman on the inside. This is just as much as how a woman looks and feels on the outside. I hate to see women look in the mirror and talk negatively about their appearance. It bothers me when ambitious, goal-getting women have difficulty feeling powerful in even the most elegant outfit because they don't see themselves as powerful. I want women to grow throughout the journey of self-discovery, unpack their insecurities, and look at themselves with the beauty, strength, and confidence that God gave them.

Imagine if more women took one step to increasing the love they have for themselves. This is only one step to showing up with power in the way they walk, talk, and dress. Think about what our workplaces and communities would look like if every woman exuded power and confidence with her style and was not afraid to stand out.

My goal for this book is to elevate your way of thinking about your purpose, the things that are stopping you from being your best self, and the power God gave you. I will challenge you to think deeply about the areas of your life that are preventing you from showing up as your full self. By the time you're finished reading, you will be able to identify self-limiting beliefs and strongholds, as well as transform your way of thinking about your self-image. You will be equipped with ways to shift your mindset about how to approach your getting dressed routine, so that you can exemplify confidence in your style. The topics we will cover may be challenging, but they will also be enlightening.

I promise to take you through the various circumstances that we, as women, typically encounter throughout life and how to overcome them. I'll do this while applying the same thought process to how you choose to get dressed and show up with confidence. I promise to be transparent and straightforward with sisterly love while igniting a breakthrough in one or more areas of your life.

Can you promise me something? Take every bit of advice, inspiration, and guidance and immediately apply it to your situation. Set aside quiet, undisturbed time to really dig into the Reflection sections. This is where you get to use what you have read and make it practical to your own circumstances. By reading the pages of this book, you'll become more self-aware of how life is used to fuel your confidence, style, and faith. Don't take this encounter for granted. Let this book awaken you to the insecurities you've faced, lift you up to fight through the strongholds, and help you get dressed according to how God sees you.

Wake Up! You Have Purpose

In 2014, I thought I had made it. At that time in my life, I felt like I had accomplished most of the things I was raised to believe would make me successful. I attended a good college and majored in a lucrative field. Then, I moved from Virginia to Texas to start working for a Fortune 500 company and was working on completing my master's program in IT project management. That same year, I married a respectable man, and we built our first home together. I thought my life was made because I had checked off the goals I was taught to achieve one by one. I was extremely proud of myself for the most part because I did what I was supposed to, giving my parents something to smile about and inspiring others by what I had achieved shortly after leaving the nest. Life was good...

...until I got laid off.

I would be lying if I said I didn't know it was coming. Thanks to this incident, I learned to never be in a role or position that is not providing direct value to any company. I had just recently switched roles, and let's just say it was one of those things where I was promised one thing but received another. I was told I would be able to broaden my career and take on more project management work, only to learn that I would be stuck doing mind-numbing administrative tasks that did nothing for the company's bottom line. While among my team, I felt something coming. I knew something was wrong in my gut. At 27 years old, I never thought I would experience the type of rejection that sunk me into a deep, unknown hole.

I got the degree, and I did a great job at work. Why didn't they want me?

I did everything I was supposed to do. What now?

I never liked rejection. In an instant, the elimination of my position made me feel like my worth was gone. I felt useless, powerless, and valueless. All of these emotions hit me at once—hard. Just when I felt like I had life figured out (as much as a young 27 year old woman could), I lost the two prideful things I used to identify who I was—my career accolades and security. Per the norm in corporate America (and by the grace of God), I ended up landing another role in a different department. Although I didn't miss a beat financially, the entire layoff situation replayed in my head multiple times a day. I became extra paranoid and self-conscious at work.

Are they about to eliminate this position, too?

Did I say the right thing in that meeting?

Did I make a mistake?

I was on pins and needles trying to be extra careful and diligent with the goal of dodging another moment filled with humiliation and rejection. Being on edge like this really got to me. I knew I was worth more than a number on someone's budget sheet that will be removed as soon as the higher-ups needed to "reduce costs." I didn't deserve to walk around feeling like this, so I refused to settle for this type of unfulfillment until I could retire. I began having more and more quiet times with God. I removed any distraction that wasn't feeding me with positivity or inspiration. Each day, I became still and sat at God's feet. I had so many questions that no corporate manager, friend, or family could answer. I needed the source of strength to strengthen my weaknesses and reveal my purpose to me.

Day after day, I studied the Bible, journaled, prayed, and listened to worship music while waiting to hear from God. At that time, I had no clue what His voice sounded or felt like, but I knew I was in a vulnerable position—only He could provide comfort. One day, during my quiet time with the Lord, something strong hit my spirit. I heard God say, "This is your wake up call. Don't you think I have more for your life than a job that comes and goes, a status or title that can change any day, or material things that have no value?"

I thought, *Wow! Ok God, You have my attention.*

The Lord said, "There's more I have planned for you. Do a prom drive for high school girls."

Umm, come again?

I had no clue how to organize a prom drive (and at that time, no desire to do it). But God told me to, so I obeyed. When we pray for God to reveal something to us, we must be prepared for His response.

Not having any expertise, very little resources, and no experience at all, I held tightly to the Word of God and my desire to tap into His real purpose of my life. The prom drive plans were quickly underway. My excitement grew as I started mapping out everything. I identified a local high school that would benefit the most from the prom drive, set up meetings with school administrators, and titled the event, "Embrace Your Crown." It was such a fitting name for the love I would pour into the young ladies as they prepared for their prom night.

To make myself feel fancy, I had a coworker design a quick flyer to advertise the need for prom dresses and accessories. Weeks later, I started receiving shipments of beautiful formal gowns, shoes, and accessories from family, friends, coworkers, and strangers who wanted to donate to the cause. Within a few months, I found myself teaching, inspiring, and giving back to young girls who simply needed someone like me to understand them. This was when I knew I was called to be something greater. The amount of joy, peace, and fulfillment I received from working with these young ladies was a clear sign that I was walking in the right direction.

About a year later, I filed the paperwork to turn Embrace Your Crown into a 501(c)(3) organization. This nonprofit gave my life new meaning.

I gained confidence about how God sees me by serving others. Before I could truly process the shift that was happening within me, I started hosting events, had an official logo created, started selling branded merchandise, expanded to work with another high school, and even tapped into the world of public speaking.

Embrace Your Crown, an organization that started out of a small act of obedience, gave me the courage to trust God more when He gave me bigger assignments. The influence that I always had, but didn't know existed, grew because I decreased myself and allowed God to increase His presence in my life. By doing this, I learned that purpose has nothing to do with your career, status, title, or even passion. Your purpose is the unique God-given gift that serves others. Purpose cannot be controlled by anyone else. Purpose is soul-led and always aligns with God's will.

The concept of purpose gets everyone in a tizzy because, if they haven't found their reason for living at the specific time they *think* they should, they give up and assume the world has no need for them. In today's media-driven world, we see people accomplishing goals, impacting lives, and doing "what God called them to do" as they constantly release their curated messages to the masses. But here's the thing… most people haven't fully reached their true purpose yet. They're just doing their part by serving on the journey to discovering their purpose—the reason why God made them. And that one reason may not be realized immediately.

We've made purpose into something that seems complex or difficult to obtain. We read books, attend church services, and go to events to receive a feel-good message about how to find our purpose. There are a lot of people who make a living off of helping you find your purpose, and I'm not knocking them. But what I will tell you is that excluding the key player—the Creator—from your quest for purpose, will lead down the wrong road.

A quick search of the word will give you this definition:

purpose [pur-p*uhs*][1]
noun
1 the reason for which something exists or is done, made, used, etc.
2 an intended or desired result; end; aim; goal.
3 determination; resoluteness.

It's a straight-to-the-point definition, right? But it's missing something. According to God, your purpose is the intention and plan He has for you that is <u>aligned with His purpose.</u> God always has a goal or a purpose that is related to what He does in the world. Every person, every situation, *everything* is a result of God's will.

I used to think that purpose meant doing whatever made me feel happy and fulfilled. While, yes, to a certain extent that's true, it's not all. The result of purpose is doing what God intended, regardless of whether it makes us happy or not. The reason I say this is because,

---

1 "Purpose." *Dictionary.com*, Dictionary.com, 2020.

as humans on earth, we have access to a lot of things that make us "happy" but are not always the best for us (i.e. not aligned with God). This superficial happiness comes in the forms of clothes, cars, homes, titles, and status.

Let's quickly relate this to your wardrobe. I consider myself to be a retail therapy queen. I can shop the best styles and deals in my sleep! A lot of women are able to do this, too. But one thing I've noticed is that most women shop for clothes that serve no purpose and just leave them in their closets. Maybe it's the high of scoring a bargain or the temporary satisfaction of adding something stylish to your wardrobe, but the purpose of your wardrobe is to serve you in the most confident way according to your personal, unique style *right now*. If you're buying clothes, shoes, and accessories "just because," with no true intention, you'll soon find yourself with a cluttered closet full of things (distractions) that no longer serve you in your current season of life. Then, after taking the time to purge your closet so that it can look practical again, you fall into the same cycle of purposeless shopping.

Does any of this sound familiar?

The same thing can occur with your life's purpose. You have to remove the distractions that are preventing you from confidently serving in your ordained purpose. But before you do that, there are some fundamental aspects of discovering God's purpose for your life that are rarely discussed but extremely important.

Don't rush the process.

One of the hardest things for people to realize is that everyone is on a different journey. God is orchestrating the specific purpose of billions of people on this earth. Do you think He would allow everyone to be on the exact same journey at the exact same time? That's impossible. When you see other people impacting lives, making a difference, and being joyful about what they're doing, keep in mind that you don't know what occurred on their journey before getting to that place in life. You don't know what they had to sacrifice or go through to get there. And let's be honest, you probably wouldn't be able to survive what they endured, so appreciate your process and ride the wave.

Don't rush discovering your purpose because you may not be ready. Stepping into your purpose prematurely can hurt you and others. If you're not mentally, emotionally, or spiritually prepared, you can inflict ungodly things into the world that go against the reason for your purpose in the first place. Take a step back, relinquish your controlling habits, and let God mold you into the woman you need to be to receive and execute your purpose.

Create capacity for God.

This is a step that cannot be skipped. When you truly want to unlock your purpose that God (and God alone) has created for your life, you have to go to Him for the revelation. God simply wants your "yes," which means you're opening yourself up to more of Him. Your "yes" means you're letting go of the things, people, and habits that no longer serve God and replacing them with His Word. He wants to reveal your purpose to you, and He does it when you're ready, listening, and available to Him. God needs your attention so that He can start shaping you into a woman aligned with His purpose.

Getting laid off from my first "big girl job" was God's way of getting my attention. He needed me to slow down, become humble, and realize that my value was more than a number on a corporate roster or material achievements. He had to let something unfortunate happen to draw me closer to Him. So, I sat and devoted my time to Him. I prayed, worshipped, and dug into His Word to receive the Spirit. I literally had to surrender control of my life for Him to reveal the true plans He had for me.

If it wasn't for my layoff, I wouldn't know the power of listening and obeying God. This leads me to my next point …

You have to do something.

We have to stop assuming that our purpose will fall out of the sky and into our laps. It doesn't happen like that. You have to take action. Some of us sit waiting for something miraculous to happen, ignoring everything God told us to do, then become disappointed when we don't know why we were placed here on this earth. Well, I know one thing is true—you weren't placed on earth to just sit and do nothing.

As believers, we're called to serve. You may not know who or what, but the only way to find out is to get out there and try. Leave your confined comfort nest, break the habit of excuses, and take that first step. Was I scared to put myself out there for the prom drive? Yes. Did it turn out exactly how I had envisioned? No. But by doing something different and taking action, it evolved into a full non-profit. The first Embrace Your Crown event inspired many women, but it mostly gave me the confidence I needed at the time. It saved me from the limiting thoughts I once believed and opened my eyes to what was possible. It expanded my territory of impact by creating a community of women who are seeking to gain confidence. If it wasn't for that small prom drive, I wouldn't have known the power God has given me to influence others according to His Word.

You have power.
You have a purpose.
You have influence.

But you will not discover it by being stagnant. Get to moving!

Don't ignore your past experiences.

I've lived with resentment about my mom's death for decades. She passed away from breast cancer when I was eight years old, and as a young girl, I never really understood why. I always asked myself why other girls had their mothers. I didn't understand what it really meant to die. I was too young to understand, but I knew for sure that I was confused, disappointed, and bitter about not having my mother. As a result, those feelings made me reluctant to talk about my mother with other people. I was never ashamed of her, but I had made up in my head that I would be judged if I told anyone. I also didn't want to hear other people's responses of pity and sympathy because it actually made me feel like something was wrong with me.

Without realizing it, I spent many years running away from acknowledging this huge part of my life. After some time, as I grew older, I started to become more in tune with my mother and who she was. I wanted to spiritually feel her more and connect with her in heaven. I told my therapist the thoughts I had about my mom and how I neglected to talk about her with others. At that time, I searched hard for more of her—to connect with her again. My therapist told me to write a letter to my mother saying things that I wanted her to know. I was reluctant to do this at first because I was afraid to open this wound, but I knew it had to be done.

On the brisk autumn morning of my 31st birthday, I sat on my front porch and wrote my first letter to my mom. I didn't try to control what the letter said—I just let God do the writing. Whatever He downloaded in my spirit was what I wrote. To be honest, I don't even remember writing most of the letter. But at one point, I looked down and God had revealed more about my purpose. I knew He had called me to help women gain confidence, but writing the letter to my mom showed me that my purpose was directly aligned with my mom's spirit. Everything I do to better women—Embrace Your Crown, style coaching, speaking, mentoring, writing this book—is a reflection of my mom. I'm continuing her spirit on this earth.

If I hadn't been obedient in writing that letter, giving up control, and letting God do the talking, I wouldn't have gotten a deeper understanding of why I exist. It was hard to revisit those moments, but it was a part of my healing. And now I'm strong enough to share this story—my mom's legacy—with women all over.

Your purpose may be a result of you healing from a past situation. I'm a true believer that everything happens for a reason because I know that God doesn't put us in hurtful situations for nothing. Your purpose is what you will struggle for. Are you willing to suffer to let God flow through you and reveal the plan He has for you? He knew when He would call my mom home to be with Him. He also knew the struggles I would face because of that, yet He strategically set up situations and opportunities to get me to become the woman I am now.

Stop running from your past. Stop trying to hide out of fear of feeling those hurtful moments again. If you're not willing to suffer, you're not willing to manifest what God has for your life. Those seasons of suffering have shaped you into the woman you are today. You believe certain things, value one thing over another, and have specific morals because of them. It's all a part of your truth that no one can take away, so it's your responsibility to own it and let God use your experiences to lead you to your purpose.

Your purpose is one overarching theme.

I have the gift of helping women feel and look powerful in their clothes. Is that my sole purpose? Absolutely not. I have the gift of listening to women and providing sound advice. Is mentoring the only thing God placed me on this earth to do? No! It's important to know that your purpose is one overarching theme with many gifts, talents, and tasks assigned to you under it.

God has many facets to Him—more than you can ever imagine. We will never completely understand or begin to comprehend everything God is and can do. And He made us the same way. We have, and will discover, multiple purposes in life that are aligned with God. Consider a diamond, for example. If you look closely, a diamond has many flat surfaces that make up it's geometric shape. Those flat surfaces are called facets, and those facets are what make the diamond sparkle. No matter how you hold a diamond, you're going to see many facets that make up the precious stone. If God gave us this stone, something that started deep in the earth with many facets that make it one of the highest coveted pieces of jewelry, why wouldn't you think He would make you, His daughter, the same way?

A diamond can be passed down through generations. This is similar to how the things you do in the world can impact the legacy you leave.

You are a diamond intricately created by God. We all have things about us we may not necessarily like or consider boring. For example, I don't think I have the best speaking skills. Sometimes my words get jumbled and I'm terrible at using fancy vocabulary. But I know God created me to use my voice to give life to others. No matter how you may feel about the "boring" or not-so-great characteristics you possess, they all work together. He made you with many facets—enough to make you sparkle at all times. It's tied to the overall reason why He created you.

When I stop to think about it, my facets include being a style expert, founding Embrace Your Crown, Inc., speaking at events, mentoring women, and being an author. It's hard for me to limit myself to one of these because they all bring me joy. All of them tie into my theme in life, which is helping women gain more confidence. You don't have to limit yourself to one thing to get true fulfillment in your life. Your talents and gifts will work together to leave a mark on the world.

I challenge you to take the time to break down your many facets and identify if they all have a common theme.

It's not about you.

Seeking purpose has made us a bit selfish. We spend so much time trying to discover what we can do to feel like our lives are not a waste. The truth is that finding your purpose has nothing to do with you. It has everything to do with the people God assigned under you. It's a beautiful thing to know that God strategically set aside a specific group of people for you to impact.

Everyone has the power and authority to significantly influence others. Your purpose starts in the world around you. You influence your children, colleagues, church family, community, friends, and lots more. By walking, living, and executing in your purpose, you begin to influence others to work towards discovering theirs as well. If one person inspires the next, who then inspires the next, then soon we'll be a generation of believers who are obedient to our assignments.

As much as it pained me to lose my job, it was the catalyst that pushed me closer to God and understanding why I was created. I'm so grateful for that. There are people who leave this life without tapping into their callings and experiencing true fulfillment. I knew early on that I didn't want to be like that. I don't want that for you, either. In order for God to give you abundance in every area of your life, He wants you to be obedient to His instructions. Give God your "yes." Make yourself available and surrender your desire for purpose unto Him. He wants to take you on a journey of being completely fulfilled and joyful. God isn't asking you to be fully prepared or have it all together. He just wants you to be willing, open, and available to Him.

Reflection

I don't want you to walk away from this chapter overanalyzing how to discover your purpose. Remember God is not a God of confusion, stress, or overthinking. He's a God of peace, so it's important for you to find the peace within yourself and in Him. Only He can give you exactly what you need to walk in your purpose, and I certainly don't want to overstep that. But I would be remiss if I did not at least give you a method to start the process of defining your purpose for yourself while you partner with God to execute it.

Consider identifying these three things to begin discovering your purpose:

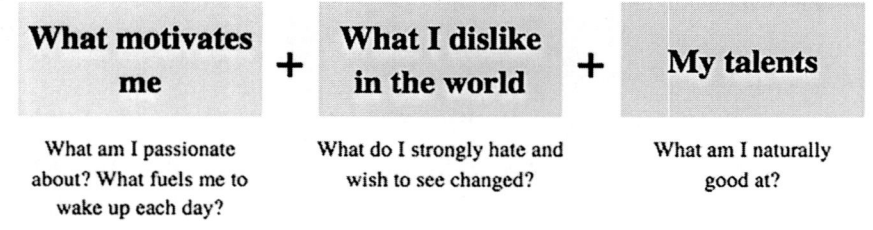

What motivates me	+	**What I dislike in the world**	+	**My talents**
What am I passionate about? What fuels me to wake up each day?		What do I strongly hate and wish to see changed?		What am I naturally good at?

= PURPOSE

Wear Your Fears

More than 20 years ago, I remember being backstage with about fifteen other 10-12 year olds ready for our cue to take the stage during dress rehearsal for a fundraiser pageant at a local high school. We were raising money for a community organization. Whoever collected a certain amount of money from selling program ads received the most recognition at the end of the pageant. To this day, I remember the big white T-shirts, sheer red tights, and white high-top sneakers we wore for our opening routine. I always enjoyed dancing, and I sometimes used it as an outlet at this young age. I was excited about this opportunity because it gave me a chance to spend time with my friends and possibly meet others.

During our break, all the girls congregated backstage to chat and have a typical tween conversation. Well, the other girls talked—I stayed quiet, as usual. I was super shy then and held everything in. An older girl, the one who led the huddle's conversation, looked at me with a slight grin and asked me something related to the jovial discussion.

After I responded, the group of girls started to laugh at my response. As feelings of embarrassment arose, questions started to form in my mind. *What are they laughing at? Did I not say the right thing? Was my answer not "cool" enough?*

On the outside, I laughed it off, shrugged my shoulders, and continued practicing for the pageant. On the inside, I made a promise to myself to never speak up again because I was afraid people would laugh or make fun of me. At 10 years old, I had no clue how that single moment would embed feelings of fear that would impact me for decades.

Reflecting on that moment made me think of experiences that teach us certain fears. I once read a CNN article that explained the two types of fears we carry: innate fears and learned fears.[2] Innate fears are the ones we're allegedly born with, like the fear of falling or loud sounds. Think of an infant becoming startled by a loud noise or sudden movement that feels like they're falling. Learned fears are the fears we're taught over time, including common phobias (fears of spiders, snakes, heights, etc.). I'm sure there are tons of scientific explanations for all of this, but one thing I know for sure is that God's Word comes before anything a person studies.

I first began to know God for myself during college. During that time, I found myself in situations that caused fear to develop within me. I stumbled on Deuteronomy 31:8, and it resonated so much that I've always held it close to my heart. In fact, I printed the verse out and

2 *What is the science behind fear?* Nadia Kounang, CNN, October 2015.

taped it on my college bedroom wall; that same printed piece of paper is still on my mirror at my parents' house.

"The Lord is indeed going before you - he will be with you; he will not fail you or abandon you. Do not be afraid or discouraged!"

- DEUTERONOMY 31:8 NIV

It's clear that God commands us to not be afraid, which contradicts any article that says we were born with fear. Did you know the phrase "fear not" is used over 80 times in the Bible? God didn't create us to come out of the womb afraid. Fear is something that we were conditioned to have or believe in based on past experiences, trauma, or things people have projected onto us.

That quick moment during the pageant rehearsal lingered in my subconscious for years. I don't believe anyone, especially at that age, wants to be laughed at or embarrassed. To prevent that from happening in the future, I silenced my true voice. I became more shy and afraid to speak up for myself because I didn't think my voice had power. That one experience made me feel like my voice and words weren't important. It made me doubt what I had to say. Even in school, I never raised my hands to ask questions in class because I was afraid my question or thought wasn't worth being heard. As a little girl, I learned how to silence my voice because of a fear that I would be judged or criticized. And ironically, no matter how you see me now, an aspect of this fear is still in me.

Can you relate? Maybe, like me, you were laughed at for something you said? That could be the reason why you have the fear of speaking in front of an audience. If you played a sport as a child, were you told you weren't that good? Did you make a wrong play that cost the game? As a young child, did you have a sense of failure that continued into adulthood? All of these experiences have the ability to contribute to our fears and teach us about our worth at a young age.

I recall countless childhood memories that continue to remind me that I was not born to be afraid. We have fears now, as adults, because of things that happened to us in the past. Children are bold, at least I know I was. When I was five, I wanted to know what it felt like to iron my hand, so I placed a smoking hot iron on the palm of my hand. I had blisters for days! When I was six, I wanted to see if I could dart across the street on my bike in front of an oncoming car without getting hit. One day, while riding bikes with my cousin, I pedaled my bike quickly to get in front of a car that was speeding down our street. Fortunately, I made it across the street unharmed. When I said I was bold, **I was bold**. Yet, as a full grown adult, I've inherited fears that have diminished my courage.

Can you remember a moment when you were a child and did something that was bold?
Do you ever wonder what happened to that little girl?
Where did her courage go?
Did past experiences teach her to be afraid?

We have to unlearn the fears that we wish to get over now as adults. You may have a fear of failure. You may have a fear of uncertainty. But do you want to leave this earth knowing you didn't do everything you were capable of because you were scared?

Just some questions to ponder on.

If you're like me, you may have given fear unnecessary power for most of your life. It makes us procrastinate with certain tasks, disobey the things God tells us to do, and become stagnant.

There are a lot of people who prefer to stay in their comfort zones. I get it. It's safe and secure. It's predictable. But these same "comfortable" people usually desire more. They want to reach new levels in life and live with a sense of fulfillment. Your desire for wanting more out of life is blocked by your submission to fear. Fear has a unique way of making us remain in situations, relationships, jobs, partnerships, and lifestyles because the uncertainty of something else makes us feel uneasy. It stops us from moving forward in life to welcome what God called us to do and become.

If you tune in to some of the most popular women's empowerment platforms, you may hear the word "fearless" being thrown around and used to describe how we should be. But sis, can I be honest with you for a second? Regardless of what your favorite motivational speaker or inspirational Instagram meme might say, there is no such thing as being "fearless." There has always been fear in our lives. And there will always be fear, *as long as we allow it*. If we continue to let our past experiences impact how we view life (or the things that we're supposed to go after), we will always be afraid.

Think of something you've attempted to do in the past. You felt like you failed at it (according to **your** standards), so now you won't even consider trying it again. Think of all the times people told you to show your talents to the world but you continued to hold back because you were afraid to "put yourself out there."

If you want to really live in the abundance God promised, you have to remember He didn't give us a spirit of fear—people and experiences did. And as long as you submit to fear caused by people or unfortunate experiences, you are not living for God. You're living for something driven by the enemy.

I've been working in corporate America for over 10 years now. After a while, I can't help but realize that I can apply some of the same professional techniques, strategies, and methods to my personal life. One day, I was sitting in a process improvement training class. I have to admit, I wasn't excited to be stuffed in a windowless conference room for two days for yet another boring training, but I complied. The instructor had the class go through a "why" exercise to help teams get to the root cause of an issue within a given process. If a certain part of our process wasn't working as effectively as we wanted it to, we had to ask ourselves a series of "why" questions to assess what was causing the challenges. Why is this an issue? Why is this happening? Why? Why?

Why?

After that training, I started to ask myself "why" to improve my own life. It allowed me to be extremely centered with myself and seek my own answer to the new things I was discovering about myself. In order to really improve something, you have to find out why it exists in the first place. I started with my personal fears that were holding me back. By getting to the root of my "why," I learned that I was a people pleaser. I struggled with saying "no" and required praise in order to feel good about myself. I minimized myself to make sure I didn't disappoint people.

Why?

Because I didn't want their feelings to be hurt, even though I wasn't getting what I needed emotionally. I often sacrificed my emotional well-being to protect others' feelings.

Why?

Because if I hurt their feelings, they'd be upset with me. And I didn't want that.

Why?

Because, at that time, my value was validated based on whether people liked me.

Boom! There it was. The root cause that was producing these fearful habits was now exposed. I was facing it head on. After, I had to unpack why I placed value in other people's emotions toward me. Inner healing was needed. That usually starts with addressing fears and habits caused by our learned fears.

A common habit a lot of people learn to adopt is overthinking. I know this is something I do more times than I like. There are times when I sit and overanalyze a recent encounter or situation, nitpicking every detail in an attempt to either control the outcome or dwell on what could've been done differently. Overthinkers usually spend a lot of time worrying about things they cannot control—they ask a lot of "what if" questions. *What if this doesn't work right? What if I do something wrong?* This usually prevents any forward progress, halts decision making, or causes actions to become paralyzed.

If you're a certified overthinker, you most likely can pinpoint the times you stopped making progress in completing a goal or plan because you thought about it in so much detail that you ended up psyching yourself out of doing it. Analysis paralysis is a real thing. I often see the same habits with my clients when deciding what to wear to work, important events, or casual outings where they want to really look good. They overthink and doubt their ability to be stylish.

Will I look good in photos?
Does this look cute on me?
Is this trendy or "in"?
Does this flatter my body?

If you're not confident in your style or aware of how to dress for your body type, the fear of not looking good will crowd your mind and cause you to overthink about your appearance. If you're not careful, these thoughts can consume so much of your mind that you end up allowing your wardrobe to stop you from showing up confidently. And when you don't feel confident in how you show up, it can deter you from accomplishing goals and executing plans. Get extremely clear on your unique style by wearing what works for you and makes you feel your best. Then, stick to that over and over again until you increase your confidence in your image. This is how you work your "move forward from fear" muscle.

Instead of spending a lot of time being afraid, put more effort into moving forward with faith. I feel like when we approach a situation that we may be afraid of, we will quickly say, "Don't be afraid. Don't be afraid. Remove the fear." Then, we put a lot of emphasis on the stress and worry caused by fear. Let's place more emphasis on moving with faith. Instead of being fearless or trying to focus on being fearless, brave, or bold, focus on your faith. Faithfully move forward. Focus on what God already gave you, which is the faith and power to overcome any fear.

Sometimes when we are caught up in the things we're afraid of, we fight through them by ourselves. You are not alone. You have help. The help is the Word. The help is God. He's already equipped us with the power to break the spirit of fear and the strength to fight it. Did you know that we have the authority, the armor of God, to fight the spirit of fear? He already gave it to us; we just have to find the tools to help us fight. God will break the bondage over your life that is preventing you from accomplishing the tasks and dreams He's planted in you.

Everyone has a certain gift or talent that they are supposed to use for the kingdom of God, but a lot of people are not using theirs because they're afraid. They've never seen the manifestation of their gifts or talents done before—that terrifies them. They are afraid of being judged or criticized. Get up and get dressed in the armor of God! Bring out your authority. Bring out your power and fight your fears so that you can be who God called you to be.

Your relationship with fear is going to dictate how you live. Will you allow fear to stop you from progressing, or will you develop the courage to fight your fear with faith? Get out of the habit of allowing fear to control your life. Instead, think about what fear represents. Similar to the "why" exercise I discussed earlier, your fear will reveal something about you—a stronghold you never knew existed. It'll reveal a new area in life that requires your attention to resolve. God will show the underlying truth behind your fears to build your faith in that area of your life, but you have to be willing to uncover it. So many of us allow ourselves to become too comfortable and stagnant. I will tell you right now that complacency is not of God. He wants you to approach Him with boldness.

Reflection

What is your relationship with fear? Do you allow it to stop you from moving forward?

What fears have you allowed to take over your life?

What are some ways you can start removing fear from your life?

Use the space below to do your own "why" exercise. Let the Spirit guide you when doing this. Be detailed, specific, and open.

One's Self-Image Does Not Fit All

I'd finally done it. I remember getting dressed one morning and looking at myself in the mirror with so much admiration for the woman who looked back at me. I was proud of myself for accomplishing this goal. As I took one final look in the mirror to make sure my hair was on point and my dress fit exactly how I wanted it to, I carefully grabbed my cap and gown and raced out the door.

It was a warm, sunny Saturday in May, and I was extremely anxious to begin the walk to the arena to start marching in. Also, I was burning up as I stood under a nearby parking lot with hundreds of my fellow classmates. We walked from the parking deck, across the lawn, and into the arena to take part in our college graduation. When I walked into the ceremony, I frantically scanned the filled seats to locate my family. I had aunts, uncles, and cousins travel from out of town to witness me receive my diploma—a well-celebrated feat for my family.

After I located them, I waved with a big smile on my face, proceeded to take my seat, and released a huge sigh of relief.

I had done everything right. I majored in information technology, a field that was considered "guaranteed money," finished in four years, and was ready to take the working world by storm. The country was in the middle of a recession. Although I knew the state of the economy, I thought, *I'm good because I have an IT degree. Everyone will need me.* Boy, was I wrong. My parents told me to start applying for jobs before graduation because I was finishing up my senior year. But, due to my procrastination and naive mindset, I took the entire job application process as a joke.

As soon as I graduated and moved back home, I was faced with the pressure of becoming an actual adult almost overnight. I started applying for jobs like my life depended on it. May flew by, June passed, then July ended—I was still unemployed. Every day I woke up, hopped on the computer, and applied for jobs—any and everywhere. I was desperate. That desperation turned into depression as I watched my college peers secure job after job. I know because I saw the brag posts every time I logged onto Facebook. These were the same people I took classes with—the same people who stayed up with me in the lab to complete projects. I struggled with the fact that they were able to land a job in our field (the social proof that college was worth it), yet I couldn't even get a temporary administrative assistant job.

Not only did I watch my college classmates announce their new job offers and relocation plans, but I felt the most pressure from my parents.

"What jobs did you apply for today?"

"Did you do this or that to your resume?"

"Get up and go apply in person!"

"I talked to such and such today… send them an email with your resume."

My parents had great intentions, but their persistent urging made me feel uncomfortable. They made me feel like I needed to rush to make my own money or like I wasn't good enough to land a well-deserving job. Sometimes, I felt like I was both.

I thought I had been trying my best, but I found myself riding in the front seat of an emotional roller coaster that never stopped running. I would apply for a job I knew I was qualified for, but I'd receive an automated rejection email five minutes later. I would get a call for an interview I felt good about, but I'd never get a call back (even after numerous follow ups). That pride I felt at graduation started to fade away as I began to question if all of my hard work was valued as high as people had made it seem.

I know now that this is just one small example of how I compared my life to others. And to be completely honest, I still sometimes catch myself doing this when I see my peers accomplish the same thing I desire to achieve. When this happens, I try to think to myself, *Shaquanna, comparing yourself to others is a sure way to disappoint God.* And I refuse to do that! You and I both know that it's foolish to try to compare ourselves to the next person. Nothing good ever comes out of it—unless you've mastered the art of turning comparison into motivation (we'll get to that later). Rather, we consciously (or unconsciously) point out the similarities and differences between each other. Here are a few inherent problems with this.

1. **We compare the wrong things.**

   How often are you comparing yourself based on the material things someone has instead of their character? Are you determining someone's value only by their clothes, cars, homes, beauty, paycheck, or followers? Do you ever stop to think about that person's integrity or moral ethics?

2. **We compare our worst with another's best**.

   Are you only focusing on the "perfect" lives people choose to show or tell you and comparing that with the things you wish to obtain? How many times have you compared your chapter one with their chapter ten?

3. **We focus on the wrong person**.

   Have you ever stopped to think maybe you're wasting too much time trying to be like someone you have no business emulating? For example, are you trying to launch your career in one field and becoming upset because of someone who's thriving in a completely different area?

Don't be the woman who robs herself of a content life by creating the unhealthy habit of comparing your life to others. Comparison leads to jealousy and envy, causing bitterness and unhappiness. By doing this, you neglect your most valuable possession: your life. While it is difficult to eliminate comparing ourselves to others altogether, there are several practical steps to moving past it. Let's touch on a few things to remember the next time you feel the urge to measure your life to another person's.

Everyone has a struggle.

Late one night, I was doing my usual Instagram lurking and stumbled across a woman's page that immediately grabbed my attention. I honestly wish I still remembered her handle because I fell in love with her perfectly curated photos. She had a beautifully renovated house, successful career as an attorney, and gorgeous natural hair. She was in great shape and took frequent trips to some of the most exotic places around the world. As I kept scrolling down her feed, I noticed myself comparing my life to hers. I started to become unhappy with the life God blessed me with because I had caught a glimpse of this stranger's seemingly flawless life. I quickly snapped out of it, closed Instagram, put my phone away, and reminded myself that she's only posting what she wants people to see. I don't see her struggles and insecurities.

Don't compare your current reality to a perfectly curated depiction of what someone wants you to see about them. Some people show you their successes and accomplishments as a way to motivate and inspire others. However, especially on social media, a lot of people only show their "highs" to receive external validation, replacing a void they have in their own life. We cannot control what people show us in the highlight reel of their lives, but we can control our reactions, thoughts, and feelings toward them.

Everyone's journey is different.

When we compare ourselves to other people, we discount the journey God laid out before us. There are specific things God has ordained over our lives at specific times. One of my favorite chapters in the Bible, Ecclesiastes 3, states how everything happens in its own time— there is a time for every purpose and season. Nothing is exempt from that. Can you imagine a world where everyone was on the same exact journey with identical timelines? Boring! When you're at your lowest point, someone else may be at their highest. But in the next season, it may switch. You could be at your highest point when someone else is at their lowest. Ultimately, God orchestrates a specific journey for each of us that will always work together for **His** good. Don't get caught up trying to leave your lane to drive in someone else's.

Create boundaries to protect your peace.

Listen, this is a game changer. One of the key components of inner peace is setting boundaries. It's important to establish boundaries with yourself, your family, coworkers, and basically everyone. Unfortunately, it's common for women to struggle with setting boundaries to protect ourselves. For many decades (centuries, even) we have been taught to sacrifice our own physical and emotional needs for others to avoid appearing "selfish." To keep it real, a lot of the issues we face with the people in our lives are most likely due to the boundaries we neglect to set *and* reinforce.

Let's revisit social media really quickly. It has its pros and cons, but the #1 thing I dislike about social media is that it gives us yet another way to clock other people's lives to see if we measure up or not. For instance, I could be trying to pay down debt so that I can afford the house I desire. One day, I log on to Facebook and the first thing I see is someone's post with their realtor and "#homeowner" in the caption. Because I still have some ways to go before being debt-free, I am no longer content with the pace I'm moving at because someone else has done what I haven't. We shouldn't diminish what we're doing to reach our goals after seeing someone else do it before us.

As mentioned earlier, we cannot control what people share publicly on the Internet, but we can control our responses. If you're not at the place where you can manage your feelings, create a boundary until you're able to accept what you see or hear (or ignore it for that matter). You can unfollow or mute those who share information you cannot handle. Remind yourself that you're just protecting your daily information consumption. This also applies to those you know in real life. Simply put, do what you have to do to take care of your mental health.

When we compare our lives to the lives of others, we trigger our minds to think we're not good enough. We start to doubt our own abilities and worthiness. This is often the case when it comes to body image. We see it in the media, pop culture, and even our own circles. At some point, we've all been there before (if not currently still dealing with it). We see images of perfectly shaped bodies in our face each and every day, making us question our own body image. As a result, we start to develop unhealthy habits of comparing ourselves to others until it becomes normal behavior. Because of the misguided desire to be more like other women, we become discouraged when we don't meet that expectation.

In my line of work, I find that the negative emotions a woman has towards how she looks (and ultimately her self-esteem) directly affects how she dresses. One thing I see is that most women struggle to dress confidently because, after comparing themselves to others, they don't believe they are truly beautiful.

Nowadays, we often notice that women with the best bodies and cutest wardrobe get the most attention. One can begin to wonder, *Why can't I look or be like her?* Sis, let me be honest with you. What she has is nothing different than what you have. We all are born with inner confidence, regardless of how different we may look from each other. It's just up to us to remove what's stopping us from being confident so that we can shine from the inside out. Thoughts like, *I'm not ___ enough* (you can fill in the blank with almost any adjective) can instantly lower our confidence and make it harder to love ourselves. Stop putting so much energy into why you don't have what someone else has (or what you believe you deserve to have) and embrace what you do have.

Comparing ourselves to others can sometimes come naturally, but there's a thin line between comparisons that spark envy versus motivation. This is where self-awareness comes in. When you're able to detect feelings of ill will towards someone, you can fight begrudging thoughts. From there, you can identify ways to become inspired. Shift your perspective. No one succeeds when comparison is instigated by our own ego. Comparison, when made positive, can be a powerful and unstoppable motivator.

One of my favorite books in the Bible is Deuteronomy. One morning, I started reading the second chapter of the book and immediately became intrigued. In this chapter, Moses is speaking to the Israelites about their wanderings along the Red Sea through the wilderness. For me, I equate the wilderness to feeling lost and without the necessities while enduring a wild, unfavorable environment. While the Israelites were wandering, looking for something to conquer, God instructed them not to take over what was not theirs. He told them three times, "I will not give you any possession of their land."[3]

How many times have you wanted what somebody else had during a season where you felt like you were lacking? You may see what someone else has—possibly the one thing you believe will make you whole again—and feel like you're supposed to have it (or worse, take it). Because the Israealites obeyed God's instructions and didn't take over land that didn't belong to them, He ended up providing the ultimate reward at the end of their journey. The Lord destroyed the people in

3 Deut. 2:5, 9, 19 NIV

the land that belonged to the Israealites and handed it over to them. The land He gave them was **theirs**. As much as they struggled through the wilderness, enduring a season of lack, God still led them to the land that belonged to them, as promised.

When you're busy comparing yourself to the things you see others achieve and obtain, you must remember that everything you think you want may not be intended for you. It may not be what God wants for you. What He sets aside for us is far better than what we want in the first place. Just because you're in the wilderness doesn't mean you get a pass for giving in to your weak flesh. Stay grounded and obey God's commands. He will lead you to **your** land and fight for you to get it.

Reflection

It's natural for us to compare ourselves to others, but it's important to recognize when it starts to affect our mental well-being.

Ask yourself these honest questions: What area(s) of my life am I measuring against other people I know or come across? Why do I believe it's easy to compare myself to them? How has this comparison affected my self-esteem?

Let's brainstorm. List 1-2 action items you will take this week to create boundaries and protect your inner peace while moving toward the land God has set aside for you.

Unleash Limiting Beliefs from a Broken Heart

Here is where I let you in on one of the hardest and most pivotal moments of my life. Not only did it impact my relationships, but it exposed me to what I truly thought about myself.

I started college in August 2005. By October 2005, I was in a "serious" relationship with someone I thought would be my forever. Although I had boyfriends in high school I "loved" (the say-I-love-you-after-three-months-then-break-up-a-month-later type of love), this newfound college boyfriend was my first true love. We fantasized about life after college together (ok, it was mainly me). In my mind, we were going to move in together, get married, build a family, and live happily ever after. I thought I had my fairy tale life all planned out. We enrolled in the same classes and even pledged our Greek organizations together during the same semester. He was my everything. Because of that, I gave him my everything.

Although my relationship seemed like it was perfect, things took a complete turn after my then-boyfriend and I were initiated into our Greek organizations. We celebrated the fact that we had made our dreams come true together, but there was something missing. The red flags were there, and I knew there had been a change. I ignored it until he randomly broke up with me with an explanation that didn't make sense at the time. Looking back, I think the reason why I had a hard time understanding why he was ready to go was because I didn't want to believe that he was leaving me or the fairy tale love story I had created. That is, until one morning when it all came crashing down on my heart.

Coincidentally, we lived in the same campus apartment building, on the same floor, and right down the hall from each other. Not too long after the breakup and many attempts to try to make it "right," I left my apartment one day to run errands. As I walked past his apartment door to the stairway to leave the building, I heard someone coming up the steps. To my surprise, it was a woman with her hair wrapped up and slippers on wearing an oversized t-shirt. It was *his* T-shirt—one I had become familiar with from my countless overnight sleepovers.

My heart felt like fiery glass shattering into pieces. Rage immediately consumed me, and every action after that moment was made by a young woman who had been officially broken. I immediately came out of character, went to my line sister's apartment (which was also on the same floor), and expressed my anger. Then, I went to my ex's apartment to plead with his roommate to tell me what was going on with this other woman. I didn't get the answer I wanted so, in an attempt to retaliate, I ran to my apartment, put all of his clothes that were in my room into a trash bag, poured bleach on them, and left the bag outside his apartment door.

I told you, I was not Shaquanna at that moment.

Minutes later, my outraged ex, along with his roommates, arrived at my apartment door. With anger in his eyes, he confronted me about his damaged belongings. In the blink of an eye, I found myself slapping him in the face with every ounce of inner strength my soul had.

This is something I still regret doing. But when you're young and dumb in love, it unfortunately comes with the territory. Months after that dramatic morning, shattered heart and all, I still couldn't let him go. We still talked every day, had sex, fought, then became "friends" again. It seemed like a never-ending cycle. I thought that with enough convincing, if I kept showing up for him in ways he didn't show up for me, I would change his mind. We would mend everything and resume our relationship. (Side note: Ladies, you will never change the mind or heart of a man. **Never.** So stop trying.)

I lived for this man, and he knew it. He led my heart on with wishful thinking, and I allowed it. Time after time I leaned on his old promises and potential, thinking they were still valid. I placed a lot of my value and self-worth in him. I forgot who I was and everything I'd been taught. Because I saw so much of my future with him (and this was the first guy I ever saw myself with long term) I held on to what could be—this blinded me to reality.

Heartbreak happens. Sometimes it comes out of nowhere, and other times it's built up over time until the pain hits you so strong that it immobilizes you—leaving you stuck, humiliated, and confused. Not all heartbreaks are from romantic relationships. Absent fathers, neglectful mothers, toxic friendships, and even the death of a loved one can make us feel like someone who once held our hearts has ripped it into small pieces that seem impossible to put back together.

Do you want to know a secret? You can put the pieces of your heart back together again. And you will. Time heals all wounds, and it requires internal processing and unpacking to go from damaged to whole again.

Take your power back.

The enemy preys on us the most when we're hurt. A broken heart often leads to a weak mind, which causes us to question our self-worth and whether we're good enough. During my season of heartbreak, I allowed my ex to determine my value. That was the worst mistake I could've ever made. I gave this man and the devil all of my power instead of remembering the authority God gave me. You were born with the power to love yourself, regardless of what others may say or think. You have the power to know and see your self-value. You have the power to stand firmly with both feet on solid ground to show the world you are enough. That strong power is how you change your situation based on what's best for **you**.

Putting yourself first is a primary demonstration of power you can show. As women, we're quick to put everything and everyone before ourselves. Then, we wonder why we're hurt or emotionally exhausted in the end. I want you to apply a new rule to your life from this day forward: you can no longer prioritize another person's emotions or needs without receiving what you need first. By "prioritize," I mean giving too much of yourself away (your love, attention, and acts of service) to someone who doesn't reciprocate it. If you're in a relationship or situationship where your emotional needs are not being met, evaluate your position and play the smart move. Don't wait until it's too late after the damage has been done.

For some of us, this is beyond difficult. I get it. Sometimes we stay in situations where we're being hurt because it's the only thing we've seen or experienced. Other times it's because an emotional or physical need is temporarily being met. You deserve more than for pain and heartbreak to be your normal. It goes against everything God's laid out for you. Take back your power!

Let joy back into your life.

If you notice, God never said He will give you happiness. He promised joy. There's a clear difference between happiness and joy. Happiness is a temporary emotion that's usually achieved through external things like people, possessions, places, and events. Joy is an ingrained spirit of happiness that lasts forever. It's the peaceful confidence that everything is going to be okay.[4] It's not always based on something positive happening, but it has to do with the position of your heart and spirit.

After a heartbreak, it's joy that does the healing. Focus on letting God into your life. I'm not just talking about your usual Sunday service or weekly Bible study. Get to really know God for yourself. Spend alone time with Him and pray. Don't just pray when you're going through heartbreak. Pray throughout every high and low emotion. Continuously ask Him to partner with you to help you get through it. Pray for God to step in and replace your weakness with His strength to not continue the cycle of situationships, fall victim to a depressed state, or listen to self-sabotaging thoughts. Seek Him at all times.

When trying to heal from a broken heart, you'll have good days when you think things are coming together, then you'll have bad days when you feel like no progress is being made to get you back to a place of peace. But when you're connected to God, He releases joy back into your life in various ways. When I was going through the ebbs and flows of my season of heartbreak, there were days when I put a tiny bit of effort into my appearance. I wore my favorite outfit, put on a little eyeshadow, and styled my hair just how I liked it. It wasn't to impress anyone else—I did it to represent the joy I was regaining. Getting up and getting dressed to feel good means something different when

4 High, Bill. "How Do You Define Joy?" Bill High, 27 Apr. 2020.

60

you're going through the healing process because you're telling the world that you hold the power to get your life back.

Talk about it with your "person."

Being heartbroken means being vulnerable. Usually when we're vulnerable, we put up a shield to protect ourselves from hurting even more. That has been me for the majority of my life. I've always kept my true feelings to myself, internalizing my emotions and not utilizing the support around me. If you're also familiar with harboring your feelings, you know that it causes a trickle effect of negative emotions, thoughts, and sometimes behaviors that impact us and the people around us.

I'm a fan of *Grey's Anatomy* (and I'm proud to say I've binge-watched probably twelve of the sixteen seasons so far). One of the relationships I love on the show is between Meredith and Cristina. They often refer to themselves as each other's "person." No matter how embarrassing or shameful they may feel about whatever is happening in their professional or personal lives, they always go to each other to talk things out and step in to help if needed.

Find your "person." Talk it out. The one thing you cannot discredit in your life are the people who genuinely create a safe space for you to just be you. I thank God each day for the family and friends—my "people"—who've held my hand through my breakups (and everything else so far in life). God has a unique way of placing the right people in your life at the right time. Don't lose sight of that. Find your tribe of supporters that will not only ride for you, but they will pray with you and be that voice of reasoning, too. You are safe with **your** people. **You are safe.**

Surrender.

One night, after yet another attempt to make things right with my ex and not hearing the right things from him, I went back to my apartment, climbed into bed, and started sobbing my eyes out. I knew the situation had run its course, but my heart was so captivated by this man. Throughout the months of toxic back and forth, I equated my happiness and worth to how successful I was at putting the relationship back together again. Because I had invested so much energy into our relationship, only to end up humiliated, I felt like I needed to make it work to redeem myself. Every single time I thought we were taking two steps forward toward becoming a couple again, he would say or do something that contradicted my expectations.

Here's a word of advice: when a man tells you what he wants, listen. Stop focusing on getting him to say what **you** want him to say and pay attention to his clear message. It will avoid so much. Anyway, I digress. I didn't know what was wrong with me. Why was I hurting? Why couldn't I get love reciprocated back to me in the way I envisioned?

There were so many questions but no answers. I did the only thing that was left to do: pray. At that age, I didn't know the power of proactive prayer and what it could do during an unfavorable season. But at that moment, I didn't have any strength and felt like giving up. I cried out to God and surrendered. With tears flowing down my eyes I handed over every insecurity, negative thought, and pain to Him. I remember that simple prayer word for word: "God, please help me feel whole again. Please help me be loved in the way I deserve." I didn't pray for love as a way to validate who I was. I prayed for love that looked like God—the love that He promised.

Not too long after I prayed that prayer of desperation in my room, I met my now-husband. Let me be clear. I don't want you to think it was easy because it definitely wasn't the perfect love story. I brought a lot of my damaged heart into my marriage. I had trust issues, insecurities, and unresolved emotions. Even though I was over my ex, I had not been fully healed. Moving on to a new relationship or getting married doesn't fix a broken heart—it only enlarges it.

I know God sent my husband specifically to me because, throughout all the shortcomings I developed by neglecting an emotional wound, he was patient, understanding, and **forgiving**. This entire situation— one that consumed my mind for a huge part of my 20s—taught me how to submit to God, not the enemy. Imagine surrendering your broken heart to God, then He carefully molds it back into a beautiful masterpiece. You are worthy of that. You are worthy of a renewed heart.

Reflect.

A critical component of the healing process is taking time to understand the breakup and the role you played in it. God gives us free will to decide to live righteously. We often fail and fall victim to the enemy. The gracious thing about God is that He already knows we would be capable of handling the heartbreak. He equipped us with the strength and power to do so. No one can love you like God loves you. **No one**. His love is perfect, never folding, always forgiving, and constantly comforting. Be honest with yourself (and God) and assess the things you learned from having a broken heart.

You can't expect God to heal your heart if you always put Him on the back burner, never spending time with Him and becoming lackadaisical when it comes to listening to His Word. You can't play with God's presence in your life the same way you inadvertently let a guy play with your heart.

Anything that is broken can be mended. It just takes a special type of adhesive to put it back together in a bigger and better way. Heartbreaks are God's way of telling us that something better is coming. And while we're trying to still hold on to what we think we see and feel from a relationship (like how I was still holding on even *after* experiencing pain), we have to be reminded of God's greater plan.

Reflection

Think about a recent or detrimental heartbreak. What limiting beliefs have you developed as a result of a broken relationship? Have these limiting beliefs stopped you from feeling confident and powerful?

Your Style is Your Mindset

One of the biggest things I struggle with in life is imposter syndrome. My personal definition of imposter syndrome is having feelings of not being good or smart enough, even though I'm successful. I often cringe when people congratulate, celebrate, or tell me they're inspired by what I do and have accomplished. I appreciate the love—I truly do. But I sometimes feel like I'm not worthy of the success, titles, and opportunities. It's weird because, of course, I want to be successful and flourish in life. But I usually downplay or hide my brilliance and disguise it as being "humble" because I haven't really internally accepted that I am good enough. Deep, right? Don't worry, it's a recurring topic in my therapy sessions. I'm not perfect. And as much as I preach to you about being confident in yourself, I also struggle with being confident in all of my abilities.

Life has taught us to be habitual self-sabotagers. Like I mentioned earlier, our past experiences and trauma have shaped how we feel about ourselves and, unfortunately, causes us to develop a mindset of negativity instead of positivity. Recognizing when you're self-sabotaging yourself requires you to be centered in where you are emotionally, mentally, and spiritually, as well as being aware of your patterns. Unfortunately, the act of self-sabotaging has become so embedded in us that it's almost considered normal. It's not normal, sis. And it's important to start recognizing this bad habit so that you can address it accordingly.

Take a moment and ask yourself these questions:
Am I avoiding something that needs to be done?
Am I masking my emotions with excessive, unhealthy behaviors
(comfort eating, drugs and alcohol, intentionally harming myself)?
Do I have imposter syndrome?
Am I always procrastinating?

If you answered "yes" to any of these questions, you may possibly be allowing yourself to engage in self-sabotaging behavior that may be impacting your relationships, career, and personal goals.

One day, I stumbled upon this quote that gave the perfect analogy about how we should consider our thoughts.

"Your mind is a garden. Your thoughts are the seeds. You can grow flowers, or you can grow weeds."

- OSHO

Simply put, your mind controls everything—every word you speak, action you take, and moral you believe. If your mind isn't rooted in positive, beautiful flower seeds, you will produce "weeds" that prevent you from fully believing in yourself. And just like the weeds in our yards, it only takes one before millions of others quickly sprout up.

The more you plant the negative seeds in your mind, the more weeds will grow. Oftentimes, the weeds show in the form of the following:

Procrastination: Avoiding something you need to do because you're afraid of the outcome. To be transparent, I put this book off much longer than I wanted to because I was afraid of its potential impact on others. I feared managing the responsibility of using my story, voice, and expertise to transform the lives and mindsets of readers like you. Maybe you're putting off a specific task or assignment because you're afraid of the additional responsibility, potential for success, or inevitable life change. Maybe you fear not knowing the outcome. The longer you procrastinate, the longer you will be held in bondage.

Perfectionism: Oftentimes, you may procrastinate because you feel something has to be perfect before taking any action. It's probably safe to say that we've all grown accustomed to fearing failure. Because we try to control the outcome before it actually happens, we focus our energy on perfecting every detail and end up either beating ourselves up when things aren't perfect (because the saying is true, **nothing** is really perfect) or putting things off until it's the "perfect time."

Perfectionism is overrated and unattainable in most cases, so strive to finish what you started instead.

Feeling stuck: You want to move forward. You know you should. You know you have to. But you don't. While stuck, when nothing seems like it's moving, you may feel anxious and overwhelmed. Relax. It happens. It's natural. Because we always think life should look differently, we allow our thoughts to take over and stifle us.

Low self-esteem: Your view of how you think you **should** be overshadows the acceptance of who you really are. You lack self-worth and are often hypercritical of yourself. The self-defeating thoughts are on repeat in your mind, and they eventually show on the outside through how you carry yourself and your actions. Understanding the reason why you lack self-worth is the first step to inner healing.

Tending to your mind (your garden) is an all day, every day task that is often overlooked. By getting caught up in our daily routines and obligations, we fail to prioritize what is filtered through our mind, which makes us vulnerable to consuming any message—good or bad. But that's the key. You have to be aware of the messages being sent to your mind, filtering out everything that goes against who God says you are. This is the very reason why I'm consistently nurturing my relationship with God. I desire to remain true to what He's stamped on my life. Negative thoughts may never be stopped from completely entering your mind. But when you remember your foundation, it makes it easy to turn on that automatic filter when you feel yourself begin to self-sabotage.

From the very beginning, God created us in His image (Genesis 1:26). We often forget that God created us to be just like Him, not like the woman next to us or the people we follow on social media. We were made to be **just like Him**. Honor that about your life, hold it in high regard, and genuinely believe it. Think about how amazing it will feel to walk around fully confident and secure in who you are all because of **one source**. He is the source who has promised and declared that you are valuable, free, and transformed. Let's break these down a bit because I want you to remember them the next time negative thoughts try to take over your mind.

You are valuable.

One of the biggest lies we have been taught is that putting ourselves above others is selfish. In fact, making yourself the priority is one of the most loving things you can do. And there's no one in the entire world who deserves more love than you. We all have important people in our lives—family, spouses, children, and friends. If you don't see yourself as the most important person to love and value, you won't ever have the full capacity to pour into others. You have to remember the Creator knew your value before He breathed air in your lungs. He has crowned you with glory and honor. It's hard to remember that on a daily basis because we face so much that shows the opposite, but those are distractions. Stay focused on your worth, act accordingly, and you will start reaping the fruit of your value.

You are free.

There are many things that hold us in bondage and captivity. Sometimes, we don't even realize it because we're used to it or taught that it is normal. We don't know how to break away and release ourselves from the negativity in our minds.

I once met a woman who struggled to love herself because she was trapped in a cycle of pleasing people who never had anything positive to pour into her. Her mother called her "fat" and "unattractive." Men she thought loved her only emotionally abused her. And her friends frequently reminded her to be a certain way in order to fit in. Because this was coming from the people closest to her, she eventually adopted these same feelings and behaviors toward herself. She began calling herself "fat" and "unattractive," abusing herself emotionally, and disregarding her true identity by trying to be someone else in hopes of fitting in.

In order to break free from bondage, you must remember who you are in Christ, rely on God's strength (not your own), focus on His truth, and actually be willing to be set free. Once you have decided that you want to be free and healed, God will start breaking off the chains that have held you captive and begin restoring you.

You will be transformed.

As you begin to remove the self-sabotaging thoughts, you will make room for self-fulfilling thoughts. Your behaviors and how you perceive life will change all because you took steps to change how you talked to and viewed yourself. But, that transformation period is not pretty. It exposes your vulnerabilities and makes you face them head-on. It's uncomfortable, but it's enlightening, life changing, and the pure work of God. Anything done to transform your mindset is to set you up for the abundance of God's promises.

Believe that you can be delivered from the negative habits in your mind. Say "yes" to the breakthrough. Surrender your limiting habits to be free and restored. This journey is a process but, little by little, you will learn how to snap out of any degrading thoughts about yourself and view yourself with confidence, fierceness, and courage.

To begin eliminating the self-sabotaging, negative, self-degrading talks we tend to have with ourselves, develop a habit of quickly catching them as soon as they happen. There are a couple of ways to combat any negative thinking you encounter. We're going to call these your weed killers. The first way is to be persistent in being positive. Intentionally feed your mind and spirit with positive things. Recite affirmations, read the Bible or inspirational books, and listen to worship music or uplifting podcasts. You can even detox your social media feeds so that they are only full of things that will positively motivate you.

The second is to watch your mouth. Check who's around you and only surround yourself with people who meet your spiritual, mental, and emotional needs. Make sure the act of feeding yourself with positivity is a daily goal. Repeat positive behaviors until they take root in your mind (garden). When your mind is flourishing, the words you speak sound different. What you say is a direct reflection of your heart.

Believing in the self-sabotaging thoughts makes it easy for you to manifest those same things in your life. Eventually, your actions, behaviors, demeanor, and even your personal style begin to mirror what you believe about yourself. Similar to the woman I mentioned earlier who started to believe she was unattractive and not good enough, a woman's self-image can be directly impacted. If someone believes they're fat, they may start to wear clothes that make them look and feel frumpy. If someone works hard to try to fit in and loses themselves in the process, they may never know their personal style. Your personal style is just that—personal. When you get dressed with a free and positive mindset, your image will automatically show the same. The way you dress sets the tone for how you want to be perceived and, most importantly, it's evidence of the fruit from the work you put in—removing the "weeds" while pruning yourself of the negativity.

Reflection

Improving how you talk to or about yourself will enhance the overall quality of your life because you become more optimistic about yourself and your place in the world. Declaring positive affirmations each day will help you train your thoughts and make it harder for the "weeds" to enter your mind.

I adopted this method of creating relatable affirmations from Maya Elious, and I encourage you to create your own that will resonate with you. Write them down and place them somewhere you can see every single day.

List five achievements. They can be personal, professional, or style-related—really anything you're proud of.

Achievement #1:

Achievement #2:

Achievement #3:

Achievement #4:

Achievement #5:

Now, flip those achievements into affirmations.

Affirmation #1:

Affirmation #2:

Affirmation #3:

Affirmation #4:

Affirmation #5:

These are your personal affirmations to remind you of what you're capable of and encourage you to make it through the day.

Believe in Yourself Again

We often encounter people who feel lonely, hopeless, and weary. We rub shoulders with them, work with them, talk to them, and pass by them in the store, but we would never know the sadness that's in their hearts. Maybe that person is you. You may still be trying to operate in day-to-day life, putting on a mask like everything is okay but feeling like you're drowning. Depression is one of the most common mental health conditions that stops us from functioning and enjoying the simplest things in life. It can impact our work performance, personal relationships, and overall well-being.

According to Mental Health America, one out of eight women experiences depression in their lifetime, which is twice the rate of men.[5] Women face different life stressors and hormonal changes than men, from menstruation to pregnancy to childbirth and menopause. On top of that, we must endure societal pressure to be beautiful, strong, smart, maternal, funny, and "put together," without overshadowing the men around us. We're taught to look pretty and that our appearance

5 "Depression In Women," Mental Health America, accessed July 20, 2020.

is everything way before we even know who we are or develop our self-confidence. To set the record straight, when you tap into your true identity and are secure in yourself, your appearance and image will naturally show, highlighting your inner spirit before your outer looks. With all that women face in the world, it's not a shocker that many of us inevitably fall into a depressed state.

Having a depressive episode (or being in a depressed state) is not exactly the same as being clinically depressed. A depressive episode is usually short-term and triggered by a specific event, such as job-related stress, a life change, illness, or grief. If someone's depressive episode lasts beyond a 14-day period, then professionals officially classify it as depression. Depression looks different based on the individual. Not everyone has the same "be sad, stay in pajamas, and eat food all day" symptoms. Some show their depression by becoming angry or indulging in negative behaviors. Other symptoms of depression may include avoiding settings that were once enjoyable or being irritable.

I've had my own experience with various depressed states. My first experience being depressed happened the summer after I graduated from college. After college, I went back to my parents' house broke, with no job prospects, and feeling envious because my peers were succeeding post-graduation without me. For the first time in four years, I was forced to sit by myself to process my college years and face the brutal pressure of finding a job in the middle of a recession. I was consumed with sadness and hopelessness.

I experienced another season of depression in 2013. After getting married and building my first home with my husband, I started a new position at work. Yes, these were seemingly good life changes, but I didn't know how to process them. I needed to mourn what I had lost. Yes, I was happily married, but I needed to grieve my singleness. Closing on a new home was an amazing accomplishment, but it made me face a lot of my own financial vulnerabilities and responsibilities that I had never really learned. Starting a new role at work was great, but I had to grieve the comfort of my previous (and first) job in corporate America.

Before I realized I needed to properly grieve what I had lost in my season of leveling up, I had feelings of sadness that resulted in me not feeling or looking like myself. To make matters worse, I was also processing the pain from the loss of friendship I cherished. She was someone I trusted and leaned on while navigating my career and life as a new wife. I found out her morals and values were misleading as I uncovered lies that impacted me personally and spiritually.

Can you be cured from depression? Not really, but it can go into remission. There are healthy ways to cope with depression. Here are some ways I have dealt with my depression. They still apply to my life today.

Do one small thing.

Give yourself one small thing to do each day or week to move you forward in coming out of your depressed state. It can be something as simple as taking a shower. In the past, my goals were to work out twice a week or cut off my phone after 8 PM. These small things helped retrain my mind to be more receptive to developing a positive mindset.

As you become more consistent in accomplishing your daily or weekly tasks, it will be easier for you to recognize and cope with the triggers that led you down a depressed road. It's not always easy to immediately get up and do something positive for yourself every day. Most people struggle with this, depressed or not. But once you have it set in your mind that you actually **want** to be better, you will start to seek ways to improve.

Talk to a professional.

I would not be who I am, at this very moment, if it wasn't for therapy. When I was struggling with my life changes of getting married, moving into a new home, and starting a new job, I learned my employee benefits package included free therapy sessions. I thought it wouldn't hurt to try since it was free, so I immediately signed up to see what therapy was all about.

Therapy has carried me through some of the most difficult times I've faced. It helped me see past my "mess" to focus on my purpose. I truly believe the opposite of depression is recognizing and operating in your purpose. Therapy has taught me how to navigate my emotions, communicate my needs, heal from past wounds, and so much more. A good therapist helps you tear down the walls you've built and remove the mask you wear to unpack the baggage you have carried from childhood into adulthood. Because we, as women, are so typically used to hiding our emotions to take care of others, it's hard to set aside time to process our thoughts. Therapy creates space for us to express ourselves.

Create a reference wall.

Get in the habit of documenting what you have survived. Write down every struggle or issue you've overcome, no matter how small, and hang it on a wall. Document the exact date, situation, and outcome. In my closet, I have a bright neon orange poster by the door with random dates and descriptions. It contains each and every time God either answered a prayer or blessed me. It serves as a constant reminder that God is always there to comfort and take care of me. Seeing the poster instantly boosts my confidence in Him and myself. Looking at my reference wall gives me a sense of hope. I think, *If I went through that, I can go through this.* I've witnessed God's deliverance before, so I know He can do it again.

As I think about the small steps someone might take to eliminate any symptoms of depression, I realize their style or appearance may be the last thing they want to worry about. Heck, they're just trying to make it through the day. This is why it's important to lean on the strength of God and the role He plays in your life. Get dressed, but make sure to do it in His image first. Tap into the comfort of knowing that God created you with love, purpose, authority, and in His image. You are righteous, valuable, worthy, and confident.

You have to transform your way of thinking to stand on what you know so that your behaviors fall in line with that truth. During your depressed season, every day is an internal battle because you still have to show up in the world. Use your daily dressing routine as an opportunity to strengthen the belief in yourself as God's daughter. Comb and style your hair. Wear clean clothes. Put on a little lip gloss. Wear your favorite color. Do something small that will help you begin to radiate God's healing power within you.

Reflection

Brainstorm small steps you can take to retrain your mind to believe in yourself again.

Build Your Confidence Muscle

One early Wednesday morning, I drove into work stressed out. It wasn't because I was tired and didn't want to go to the office. I wasn't thinking about everything on my to-do list. I was stressed because I felt like my marriage was failing. Being Mrs. Power Struggle, I needed to control everything and everyone to get my desired outcome. I was tired and depleted. I felt lost and like giving up. When I reached the parking garage at work, I broke down crying. It was the ugly cry you see people doing when they're emotionally defeated.

In my moment of vulnerability, I remember crying to God and telling Him that I was giving up on trying to do things my way. I didn't know what else to do but cry. So that's what I did. I sat, remained vulnerable, and let it all out. I put on some worship music and had a real conversation with God. I said, "Lord, I don't know what I'm doing. I just want things to be better, but it seems like you're not here. It seems like I'm in this entire thing all alone. Where are you? What am I doing wrong?"

God's words were spoken so clearly to me. He said, "Surrender." In that moment, I lifted my hands and a supernatural experience took over. I handed every worry, fear, and sense of control over to God. This moment single-handedly changed my life.

In some way or form, all of us have a desire to control certain aspects of our lives—our relationships, households, friendships, and careers. I get it. These things bring us a sense of stability, so we always want to make sure they are going well. But have you ever wondered why we feel like we need to constantly be in control of the various moving pieces in our lives? We actually don't want control (or power), we just have the need for a **sense** of control. The feeling of "I have everything under control" is what gives us certainty and makes it easier to predict the outcome. It also provides consistency and makes things a bit more predictable. Again, I get it. But that sense of control is prohibiting you from fully experiencing God's will over your life. Sometimes we get so caught up in trying to control everything that we become fearful instead. We fear trusting anyone else, thinking outside the box, or allowing God to direct our path.

I can't count how many times I've been guilty of saying I trusted God but behaved like I didn't. We sit in church and proclaim to "let go and let God." We post scripture verses and inspirational quotes on Facebook and Instagram. We even say, "Trust and lean on God. He'll work it out," to others. But as soon as something unfortunate or disappointing happens to us, our trust in Him goes out the window. Stop only trusting God when it's convenient for you. Any lack of confidence in yourself is a reflection of the lack of confidence you have in God. When you are fully surrendered, your confidence is effortless. The way you walk, talk, and work is different. It just flows.

Once I surrendered to God, it became easier to seek Him. I took steps to get serious about Him by having dedicated "dates" with Him, converting my closet into a sacred prayer space, starting my answered prayers list (my reference wall), and incorporating more of Him in my marriage, work, and overall life. As a result, things started to take a shift. My husband and I's struggles started to fade away, and our relationship grew stronger. I started performing better at work and was able to serve my clients in a greater capacity. And I learned how to cope with challenges and issues much better than before.

Don't think just because you surrender to God that everything will be smooth sailing. If anything, surrendering to God will bring more tests and trials your way. But, through surrender, you take a step to recognize your power to fight them differently. Every season in your life will bring disappointing, stressful, and worrisome moments. That's life. It's going to happen. But we have to focus on making sure we're equipped to respond in a healthy, effective, and godly manner.

One of the main goals of this book is to help you understand how to surrender to God. I'm all about providing practical solutions for things, but I struggled with this one. Telling someone how to surrender to God is a bit difficult because the process is extremely personal—between you and God. My method of surrender may not be the same as yours. However, the Holy Spirit has led me to share some steps to take to get closer to relinquishing whatever you're trying to control and handing it over to God.

First, get out your journal or a piece of paper. You can also use the Reflection session at the end of this chapter. Write out all the things, people, and situations you're trying to control. These can be anything big or small, but I want you to get very specific here. Are you trying to control the outcome of something happening at your job? Are you trying to control how a man loves you or what he does? Maybe you're trying to get into a degree program, purchase a home, or go after a big dream and are stressing yourself out over all that **could** happen. Whatever it is, write it down freely and include specific details.

Now, this is the tough part. Going back to the "why" exercise when we talked about fear, I want you to ask yourself why you're holding on so tightly to the things you listed in the first step. What is it about each situation that makes you feel uncertain? Do you feel like you've failed in the particular area before and are trying to avoid that feeling again? Do you get anxious thinking about this situation being chaotic? Get specific with this, too, and allow yourself to be vulnerable about why you feel the need to control.

Take what you wrote and go to the place where you can have unfiltered and uninterrupted prayer with God. Ask Him to partner with you to remove the strongholds you're facing and work on you concerning the underlying reason why you need control. How you pray to God doesn't have to be formal. He already knows your heart. He just requires you to seek Him in all things. He desires your attention.

Now this is the other tough part that most of us struggle with—being still. When I say "being still," I'm not necessarily talking about literally sitting still for a certain amount of time. (Although, that wouldn't hurt!) But being still simply means not doing anything to control the situations you asked God to help you with. When you're still, you show God that you're ready for Him to take over. Do you really want to go against what you asked God to help you with? Remove any distractions that will trigger your control tendencies. Don't step on God's toes while He does the work you requested.

Incorporate more prayer, learn to hear God's voice, obey what He says, and repeat. Surrendering is a kingdom skill that requires practice to master. Once you learn how God speaks to you, surrendering becomes more natural. You'll eventually learn to discern God's voice from yours. I used to be completely obsessed with hearing God's voice because I felt like I was missing out. But I quickly realized that to hear God's voice clearly and distinctly for myself, I had to chase after Him in prayer and every aspect of my life. I soon discovered the various ways He speaks to me—writing is the main way I hear God's voice. When I spend valuable time in my prayer closet, I feel His nudge. He gives me ideas and messages to write down. This is how this book was created, by the way.

God has a message He wants you to hear but, most importantly, He wants you to obey. What He tells you to do will not always be easy, but it will be necessary. To live an abundant life according to God's promise, you have to do what He tells you to do. The more stubborn you are, the more you will struggle in a never-ending cycle of control that leaves you stressed, burned out, or disappointed.

Overall, the formula to surrendering to God is:

Bring your weaknesses to God and confess your vulnerabilities	+	Pray and be still	+	Listen to God's voice and obey	=	**Total surrender to and confidence in God**

Many women desire more confidence in different areas of their lives but find it difficult to have pure confidence in God first. You were born with confidence. No one was born underestimating their abilities. Throughout your life, you may have felt defeated enough that your inner confidence was weakened. This was just a way for God to make you realize that you can't lean on your own confidence. You have to trust in Him. Have faith in what He can do. Follow the formula for surrendering and watch God make everything fall into place in His time.

Having confidence in your image and style may feel good, but the work to get there is an uphill journey (something most people don't discuss). The confidence you desire to have is hidden in the process of surrender, which you may be afraid to enter. Yes, it's hard to let go of what we think we can fix, but remember whose hands you're putting your trust in. Don't assume your situation is too hard for God, and quit thinking you're more powerful than Him. Surrender everything to Him and let Him equip you with the strength and strategy to confidently succeed.

Reflection

Use this space to write a list of the things, people, and situations you're trying to control. Why do you feel the need to control these things? Be detailed and vulnerable. Take this to God in prayer.

You're Never Fully Dressed Without God

There's a reason why I'm not your traditional fashion stylist or personal shopper. When I first started my business, I was in my usual "trying to figure it out" phase and started promoting styling, closet auditing, and shopping services. In my gut, I knew it wasn't what I was really called to do. But I went with it because I knew wardrobe consulting was my passion. I quickly realized I didn't want to offer those services. Women paid me to shop for them, and I spent a lot of time creating their lookbooks. They loved the lookbooks, but they didn't wear anything I had put together. I went to women's houses to audit and help them purge their closets. I then suggested styles of clothing that would work best for them. Again, they loved everything I provided but didn't take any action to improve their wardrobes.

I had a moment when I thought I wasn't talented and that my gift was a joke. I thought, *Maybe you're in over your head, Shaquanna. You can dress, but you can't help other women do what you do.* I quickly snapped out of that self-sabotaging talk, sat in my office, and went through my notes for each client to identify what was missing. There was a gap somewhere that was stopping these beautiful, successful women from using what I provided them to feel powerful in their image. I was determined to figure it out.

After some quiet time with God, He led me to write down in my journal. I wrote, "Pray for every woman you speak to." After that day, before meeting with clients, I got quiet and prayed for their hearts, as well as their physical and mental well-being. I asked God to give me the words to say that they needed to hear. My only focus was to be a vessel of God's love to serve each and every woman in the best way possible.

Things started to shift once I brought more of God into my business. I soon realized that my true area of impact was not in clothes shopping for women, and it wasn't in styling women for events. That was very temporary and didn't give the ladies I worked with the value I knew I could offer. I wanted to be able to pour my everything into these women to identify exactly what was holding them back from feeling confident in who they were, while transforming how they saw themselves in the mirror.

Most women underestimate the power of getting dressed. It's much more than putting on a cute outfit. It can give you a boost you never knew you needed. I often say getting dressed saved me. From the time

Teaches others how to approach you

When you're getting dressed to represent God, display who you are, and declare how your day will be, you are automatically showing others how to approach and respect you. It's not a secret that when you take yourself seriously, others will take you seriously as well. We shouldn't treat a person a certain way based off of their clothes. However, it is in our human nature to form an initial opinion about someone based on what they are wearing and the image they portray. I'm not saying it's morally right, but it's human. If you're anything like me, you prefer to be treated with respect and taken seriously. Use your style to demand everything you deserve.

Throughout this book, we've covered the various areas of life where we may sometimes feel broken and hopeless. Let's use our imagination for a moment to illustrate how God uses our unfortunate circumstances for the better. Think about a small animal statue, like a kitten. You know those small figurine statutes that someone may have on their mantle at home or in their garden? Yes, imagine you're one of those right now. As you sit on the mantle day after day, you collect dust and start to wither away. Your paint starts to chip and your color also changes. One day, someone accidently knocks you over, so you have a few scratches or bumps. Little by little, you're breaking down on the outside and, inevitably, on the inside. Then, something happens and you end up being broken into small unmanageable pieces. You're no

95

longer able to stand on your own. You look around and all of your pieces are fragmented, and you no longer know what to do to put them back together again.

Now, think about the shattered pieces of the animal statue as your torn and ripped apart heart. The small pieces may also be a result of your negative self-talk habits catapulted by the fear you carry within. They could also represent the pain felt from depression and the desire to discover your purpose. When you look at your broken pieces on the ground, they remind you of your deteriorated self-esteem after countless attempts to compare yourself to the other figurines around you. Maybe these pieces of yours have been broken for a while, but they were lightly held together by a false perception of who you thought you truly were. No matter what these small pieces may represent, you realize you don't have the glue to put them back together again. You may have tried to glue your pieces together, but you ended up being broken again—going through cycles of quick fixes, only to break even worse the next time. During these quick fixes, you rushed the process to resolve whatever you thought was wrong, only to find out you didn't look any better than before.

But, then God…

Your creator, provider, healer, and waymaker entered the scene. The only one who holds the glue to put you back together in the way you should finally comes to your rescue. But the "glue" God holds is not like the ordinary glue you've been using. See, while you were rushing and worrying, trying to put yourself back together so you could "feel like yourself again" and go about your business being the cute kitten figurine, God was taking each of your pieces and restoring them into something greater. You may think you want to continue being a kitten, but God is putting you back together as a **lioness**.

Since God is the only one with the access to anointed "glue," that means He's the only one with the power and authority to take your broken kitten pieces and make you a bigger, badder, powerful, resilient, fierce, bold, worthy, and confident lioness. As a lioness, you have a renewed strength to fight and overcome battles that the kitten could've never handled. The lioness statue stands tall, holds more value, and makes her presence known. She's brave, unstoppable, and more attached to God now because she is secure in everything He has given her.

My sister, I commend you for taking this get up and get dressed journey with me. I have shared many of my most vulnerable experiences to illustrate the importance of getting dressed in God's image first. I want you to take everything we have covered and reflect on your own experiences. Ponder on what getting dressed according to God really means to you. When you put action towards instilling more God in you, it becomes easier to look at yourself in the mirror and see the woman God created.

I bind anything the enemy uses against you to dismantle the love you have for yourself. When you're facing your seasons of distress (because you will face them), stay rooted in who God says you are. As you're picking out clothes each day and shopping for new items to add to your wardrobe, remember you belong to God.

Surrender your fears and allow God to put you back together again, completely trusting that He will continue to build you up into a lioness. He knows your heart and sees everything you go through. All He wants is to see more of Himself in you—in the way you carry yourself, your image, style, relationships, and life.

You are valuable.

You are worthy.

You are bold.

You are confident.

You are safe.

Now, **Get Up** and **Get Dressed**.

YOUR NEXT STEP...

Let's connect your power to your style.

If you...

- Struggle with putting together a look that shows your personality
- Don't know where to start when identifying your personal style
- Spend a lot of mental energy trying to find something to wear

Download your free copy of

"4 Things You Must Know to Identify Your Power Look"

This bonus guide includes examples of power looks you can use as outfit inspiration, my favorite style tips, and practical tips to start power dressing immediately.

Grab yours today!

WWW.SHAQUANNACHAPPELLE.COM/POWERLOOK

I want to hear your thoughts!

What was your biggest takeaway from
Get Up and Get Dressed?

Leave a review on